Freedom to
ROAM

FREEDOM PRESS publishes *Freedom* fortnightly, *The Raven* quarterly, and anarchist books and pamphlets (currently seventy titles in print).

Freedom is a propaganda newspaper, commenting on world affairs from an anarchist point of view. The first edition appeared in October 1886. Its style has always been discursive, seeking to disseminate anarchism by getting anarchist ideas discussed by readers outside the anarchist movement.

The Raven is a quarterly magazine of 96 pages, dealing with anarchist ideas at greater length. Recent issues have included collections of essays on Anthropology, Sociology and Use of the Land.

Freedom Press has published books and pamphlets for more than a century. These include classic and recent statements of the anarchist case, history books, hilarious cartoon books, and anarchist treatments of particular aspects of life. The Anarchist Discussion series was begun in 1991.

Freedom Press Bookshop, open six days a week, also sells works of anarchist interest from commercial and academic publishers, across the counter and by mail order. The shop entrance is in Angel Alley, a long passage approached by a pedestrian tunnel, alongside the Whitechapel Art Gallery.

Send for a free specimen copy of *Freedom* and a list of over 400 titles, most of them post free:

Freedom Press, 84b Whitechapel High Street, London, E1 7QX.

Freedom to
ROAM

by

Harold Sculthorpe

FREEDOM PRESS
London
1993

First Published
1993
Freedom Press
84B Whitechapel High St.
London E1 7QX

© Harold Sculthorpe & Freedom Press

ISBN 0 900384 68 9

Typeset & printed by
Aldgate Press
London E1 7QX

Contents

	Preface	7
	Introduction	9
1	The Problem	12
2	Their land not our land	15
3	Forbidden Britain	17
4	The Battle of Kinder Scout	19
5	Rules or laws?	22
6	A Catnap on Catbells	24
7	Rutland or Orwell land	26
8	Don't Covet Prince's Covert	28
9	An expensive path	30
10	Our Forbidden Land	31
11	In the firing line	41
12	Walking in Waterland	44
13	Pesticides with everything	46
14	Taking the lid off Lydd	48
15	Tramping the tarmac	50
16	Greenham Common	52
17	The Lost Commons	55
18	The disappearance of Rhu Spit	66
19	About balls and pyramids	69
20	Menacing mountain hoppers	71
21	Hooper's hedge hypothesis	73
22	Don't trust the National Trust	76
23	An Obituary	78
	References	80

Illustrations

Pages 33-40

Menwith Hill (two views)

Forbidden Britain Day – Mickle Fell Co. Durham

Forbidden Britain Day – Ploughed out path near Ladbroke

Forbidden Britain Day – Shirburn & Pyrton Hills

Forbidden Britain Day – Hannifield Reservoir Point of Trespass

Footpath sign under water

Greenham Common

Pages 57-64

Faslane nuclear base

Footpath across Lydd army training ground

R.A. chair addressing rally at Milldale

Duke of Westminster Estate, Forest of Bowland

Faslane Peace Camp (two views)

RAF Lakenheath – For access pick up phone

John Bugg (centre) at RAF Lakenheath

Acknowledgements

My thanks go to Fay Godwin, the Ramblers' Association and members of Yorkshire & Humberside CND for kind permission to reproduce their photographs, however the views expressed are entirely my own.

Preface

"No man made the land, it is the original inheritance of the whole species ... The land of every country belongs to the people of that country."
J.S. Mill **Principles of Political Economy** 1848

To ramble is to wander in mind or discourse, to be desultory, incoherent or delirious, but also to go as fancy leads, to wander the countryside, to walk for pleasure. It is the latter meaning which is the concern of these essays; the right to walk without hindrance and without damage to the environment, the paths, bridleways and open spaces of the land.

There is a long tradition of demanding access to the countryside. For many workers in the grim mill towns of Lancashire and Yorkshire in the first half of this century, the thought of escape to the open space of the Pennines at the weekend was the only way to get through Monday to Friday. But the modern movement really began on a day in 1932 when the hundreds who walked on to the moors of the Peak District of Derbyshire were met with violence by the gamekeepers; some were arrested and sentenced to prison for what became known as the mass trespass of Kinder Scout. The fight to maintain and extend this right to recreational access has continued, a right which does not conflict with the other more serious uses of the land. This may not be even a minor revolt, but it is a determination not to allow landowners to obstruct the paths used by walkers. Ramblers may not have the reputation for militancy often associated with the occupants of a London squat or workers on a motor assembly line, yet private enterprise, landowners and state bureaucrats frequently conspire separately or together to attack their rights.

Although ancient rights of way are enshrined in Acts of Parliament, they exist today because people have been prepared to defy the landowners to establish their right to walk. Armed only with sticks and secateurs small groups each weekend tramp these paths for pleasure and the enjoyment of the countryside, but prepared to cut barbed wire, remove deliberate obstructions, confront the occasional angry landowner with courtesy and reasonableness, and determined to keep the paths free.

Public rights of way are often a nuisance to the modern industrial farmer who chooses to destroy hedges, cut down trees and block paths in the interests of the increased profits obtainable from large scale, heavily fertilised, monoculture farming. These essays consider such problems as seen by a city dweller who likes to escape from the noise and pollution of the town to the noise and pollution of the country.

Introduction

The fault is great in man or woman
Who steals a goose from off a common
But who can plead that man's excuse
Who steals the common from the goose
        Tickler Magazine 1821

Two relics of the past that survive today are far more important than any purely economic value they may retain. We have a 120,000 mile network of footpaths, tracks and bridleways, much older than our roads, some dating back more than 10,000 years, that criss-cross the land and which were once an essential part of the fabric of the countryside. They were the original means of communication between villages and later the way farm produce was taken to the nearby market towns. Itinerant traders used them to circulate the goods that could not be produced in the individual villages. Now lacking economic value they are constantly under threat as they stand in the way of the demands of large scale factory farming or cross parkland over which the gentrified owners would prefer to command exclusive use.

 We also have some one and a half million acres of land originally cleared of forest and scrub but, not being suitable for cultivation, was available for villagers to graze their livestock and as a source of wood and peat. This is land that probably predates the actual idea of private property, part of a communality that was destroyed during the Norman conquest of Britain when William divided up the available land (what else was the Domesday book for?) to give to his nobles as their reward for military success. The manorial system had arrived and the indigent farmers whether tenants (copyholders) or freeholders became subservient to their feudal landlord, the Lord of the Manor. Some rights to the use of the common land which had been part of the older co-operative economy survived this privatisation. It is these Rights in Common, attached to the occupants of nearby cottages or houses which, were they still to survive today, are a powerful means of keeping commons unfenced and access free.

From the beginning of the 13th century landowners began to see they would benefit from dispossessing the peasant farmers, enclosing the land and turning it over to the increasingly profitable sheep rearing. This was deemed legal provided sufficient pasture was left for the needs of the villagers. Many families during this period established their fortunes from wool. Up to the 17th century most of this enclosing of common land was achieved by agreement although they were agreements between unequals with the least able peasants finishing up with the least land to farm – and of the poorest quality. Freeholders were more difficult to dispossess but could be deprived of the use of common land for their pasture. The poorest land was enclosed to become forest for royal hunting.

As the pace of enclosure speeded up in the 16th and early 17th centuries there were widespread riots and uprisings that secure little if any space in the history books. This despite such activities being termed "making war against the king", i.e. treason, which even today is a capital offence. The newly established enclosed fields symbolised more than anything else the loss of land use by the tenant farmer. The population became split between men of property and men of none with a new class of people – the landless labourers – providing a large reservoir of cheap labour for the now increasingly wealthy gentleman farmers.

In the 18th century enclosures were being increasingly enforced by Acts of a parliament that represented more and more the interests of the new property owning class. By the end of the 18th century the landscape of the fertile midlands and the south had been completely transformed from the feudal open system to the patchwork of hedgerow-enclosed fields familiar today while the newly successful capitalists of the countryside were building their fine houses and surrounding them with attractive parkland to keep the landless outside and at a safe distance. More efficient use of land had been achieved but at the cost of human misery.

By the 19th century the landless peasant and his family or descendants were working in the mills and factories of the city capitalists and many developed a desire to return to the land, not to live and work for there was no work for them there anyway, but just to escape for the occasional day or so from the hideously polluted environments in which they had to live and work. They were not made welcome but the rambling movement had begun. People invaded the moorlands of the hunting gentry in the north that were so close to the mill towns and in the south they walked the paths between the hedges which the levellers of the 16th and 17th centuries had failed to level and which ironically we now seek to defend against the encroachment of the factory farming methods of contemporary country capitalists. But the campaign for the right to roam is not just or even primarily about the nature or even ownership of that landscape but about who shall walk on it. This simple aim can bring apolitical recreation seekers into conflict not with the small tenant farmers, but with major landowners – grouse moor owners, financial institutions, the Ministry of Defence (MOD) who control over 600,000 acres, and sadly also the National Trust (NT), the largest landowner after the Forestry Commission and the MOD, who supposedly holds this land in trust for us but does not always make us welcome.

Today the NT is run as an elitist club that has forgotten its plebeian past. It took the name suggested by Robert Hunter of the Commons Preservation Society (CPS), now the Open Spaces Society, when it was set up on 16th July 1894 by members of the CPS and Octavia Hill of the Kyrle Society (which had aims similar to the CPS) to take over land and to safeguard it in trust for everyone freely to use for recreation. Its loss of direction is well illustrated by what happened when it acquired the 16,000 acre Kingston Lacey estate in Dorset on the death of its last private owner in August 1981. Down came the PRIVATE notices. Up went the STRICTLY PRIVATE replacements.

1

The Problem

Every year some hundreds of existing footpaths are closed for ever and a few new ones opened. We are in danger of losing more and more of our rights to roam freely on uncultivated land, threatened as they are by, among others, the National Trust, British Rail, the water companies, government interference with the Forestry Commission, the military and many land owners.

Footpaths are often the means of reaching mountain, moor, down, cliff, beach or shore, of reaching the places you can wander freely. But sometimes you can't leave the path. On the 4,000 acre family estate in Oxfordshire of the eighth Earl of Macclesfield and his son and heir, Viscount Parker, who don't like ramblers, there are 400 acres of rough uncultivated downland in the Shirburn and Pyrton hills which form part of the Chiltern escarpment. When in October 1990 about 100 ramblers took to the public path that crosses this land, they were escorted by ten policemen including a sergeant and an inspector and closely watched by the viscount and a posse of his friends from the local gun-dog club, just in case anyone should try to stray from the straight and narrow.

Of course they could fence in the path, a solution that might appeal to the descendants of the seventeenth century god-fearing royalist, diarist and author John Evelyn. They continue to control the considerable estates at Wootton in Surrey where he was born and they don't like walkers either, reputedly referring to them as louts and hooligans. Unable to abolish the public path through the estate, they have done their best to isolate it with fencing and notices. Glimpses from the path reveal parkland with a river running through it, artificially dammed in several places to form surprisingly natural looking lakes. Very pleasant it looks, but it is not for walkers to enjoy.

Rights of way, of course, are a matter of class – the landowners and their rich friends from the city don't need them because they have the rest of the land to use. This is recognised across the libertarian left spectrum from the Class War anarchists, according to "Muck Spreader" writing in their journal, to the sadly now deceased *Southern Resister*, organ of the southern region CND, which devoted a page and a half in 1991 to a discussion of rights of way. From the latter we learned that the BBC Radio 4 programme 'The Archers', that signifier of middle class values, typecasts ramblers as yuppified cranks. From the indecisive middle, came a demand in *The New Statesman and Society*, under the heading 'Land Wars', to know why Britain doesn't have a general right of access to uncultivated land. Any anarchist would be happy to explain.

Ramblers' Association members, in their Forbidden Britain campaign, each year organise walks to maintain existing paths which are under threat and establish new ones. For their efforts they have been described by a regional secretary of the County Landowners Association as "a militant and abusive minority whose activities threaten ordinary people's enjoyment of the countryside". What could he have meant? Yes, access to the countryside is very much a class issue; of the fifty nine inspectors who decide on footpath closures and diversions, none is a woman, all are over 50 (45 over 60) and 38 are of the retired colonel category.

The National Trust, owning one per cent of the land supposedly for our benefit, has kept ownership of some of it quite secret, such as Max Gate and its grounds in Dorset, the home of Thomas Hardy. It often restricts access and doesn't hesitate to block rights of way for its own convenience, as it has done at Hidcote garden in Gloucester and Stourhead estate in Wiltshire where it blocked a public path with barbed wire as it entered National Trust land. And as for class, when the representative of the Open Spaces Society attended his first National Trust council meeting, he was asked why he was there ... "Isn't the National Trust rather on the fringes for you in the allotments movement?"

When British Rail proposed building a new channel tunnel rail link it promised to use footbridges and minor diversions to avoid blocking any of the seventy paths it would cross. Good, but then why did it seek parliamentary approval to close ten paths, where they cross the London-Newcastle east coast line, thus creating twenty cul-de-sacs? Such an easy way to extinguish a path with little opportunity for objectors to object and no need to build a footbridge. There are 2,000 places in Britain where paths cross rail lines, 100 of them on the east coast line, so was this just the beginning?

When land changes ownership it is a convenient time to close a path. For the new water companies opportunities for profit come from selling land free from the encumbrance of rights of access and this has already been demonstrated. I pick on Yorkshire Water for being quickest off the mark. They persuaded the Peak District National Planning Board to erect a "No entry" notice on a path above Holme leading to Wessenden Head moor and the Pennine Way, because they had leased the land to Boss North Inns for grouse shooting. But it is Forestry Commission sales of land that are now providing the biggest threats to access. Although there are no rights of way on Forestry Commission land, access is permitted and indeed often encouraged by the provision of picnic sites, car parks and nature trails, but this could all disappear when ownership changes.

Between 1981 and 1991 400,000 acres of Forestry Commission land was sold off and the "Keep off" signs erected, the forest walks closed, the picnic sites and car parks locked away. The government had plans to sell off another 250,000 acres during the following ten years including many popular recreational areas. But surely most of the nearly three million acres owned and managed by the Forestry Commission are safe for walkers? During the 1992 election campaign, did not John Major give an unequivocal assurance that the government had no intention of privatising the state forests; and didn't the Scottish Minister confirm this most forcibly in the House of Commons a few weeks later? Yes they did, but they didn't mean it. It is now clear that the Forestry Commission is to be abolished and all this land, valued at two billion pounds, sold off.

Many excuses are used to justify keeping people off the land. The military, well known as land grabbers, most ingeniously, claim that they are protecting sites of special scientific interest and, in particular, rare plants in danger of extinction. Footpath erosion is another excuse used to justify restricting access, but how widespread is it? On a recent bank holiday Saturday in May I stood on the Pennine Way above Hebden Bridge, near Stoodley Pike, memorial to the Napoleonic wars, counting the eroders as they tramped past. It was not a demanding task for in one hour there were none.

For the most outrageous proposals to date we turn to Sir

Frederick Holliday who as Head of the UK Joint Nature Conservation Committee presumably carried some clout with the establishment. His suggestion was that walkers should have to buy a ticket from the landowner to walk on his moutain, moor or footpath. Is this "fresh air tax", as it has been called, the latest idea by the authorities in their desire to control our movements? How fortunate that they cannot yet control our minds – or can they?

2

Their land not our land

In a capitalist country ownership gives control, so who owns the land of Britain? Not easy to find out, because although a central register is kept, its contents are not particularly accessible. Leaving aside that no-one actually owns land, only the freehold, defined as a property free of duty except to the crown, how much is still owned by the old aristocracy and landed gentry? Have they not all been dispossessed by death duties, capital gains and inheritance taxes; reduced to living in the servants' quarters whilst we traipse around the main rooms, having paid our two quid to the National Trust, allowed to look at but not touch the furniture and treasures?

Of Britain's 93,174 square miles of land surface, the state and public bodies control about 15 per cent. This includes 5 per cent used by the Forestry Commission sometimes to produce those coniferous deserts and one per cent churned up into mud by Ministry of Defence tanks. One per cent belongs to the National Trust who are not above selling off bits to the MOD for more tank practice or another firing range.

In a property-owning democracy with two thirds of households owning their own mortgage you might suppose that control of the other 85 per cent of land is widely distributed. But reality, as usual, is different. Marion Shoard in *This Land is our Land* quotes a survey which concluded that in 1967 a hard core of titled families – dukes and marquesses, viscounts, earls, barons, baronets and the royal family – owned over 31 per cent of the land with 200 (over two thirds) each averaging eight square miles and concludes that now, 20 years later, the situation is likely to be little different.

The Sunday Times in its survey of Britain's 400 richest people in September 1990, who between them own 6,875 square miles, or 17 square miles each, found that 103 are aristocrats, 78 with a seat in the House of Lords, and 80 gave their occupation as landowning! Of their total wealth of £54.3 billion, one third is in the hands of large landowners. Plenty here for the one third of householders who are landless.

Strangely absent from this list are the major industrialists of the 19th and early 20th centuries who made their fortunes turning British northern towns into smoke polluted slums. Because in Britain no bourgeois revolution displaced the landowning class, the old country estates remained intact. These industrialists achieved their socially upward mobility by aping not replacing the existing establishment. This involved them in acquiring their own land, sending their sons to Oxbridge to study classics instead of engineering and marrying their daughters into old money. Some economists attribute the decline of the capitalist competitiveness of British industry this century to the time these "captains" spent hunting, shooting and fishing. All this was made easier by the agricultural depression towards the end of the last century when much land went out of cultivation and rural workers were forced to the towns to find work; in the phrase of the time, the pheasant displaced the peasant. So old money joined new money, both became richer and the aristocracy and landed gentry kept much of their political power. These industrialist families may not be among the 400 wealthiest but I doubt that they need income support.

The intelligentsia of late Victorian England also joined the movement to escape the grimy towns and return to the countryside. Writers and artists, John Ruskin, William Morris and Edward Carpenter prominent among them, advocated a return to an imagined pastoral tranquillity. But it was mainly the middle classes in the south who responded, using industrial money to move out of London into the Surrey hills, creating a picture postcard parody of Robert Blatchford's *Merrie England*.

For the industrial workers of the northern towns, tied to the factory floor for six days a week by the need to make a living, escape was not so easy; except on Sundays. Then with bicycle or on foot they left behind the pollution and made for the purer air of the surrounding moors, often to find access to much of it denied by those who had got there first or had never left. But that is another story.

3

Forbidden Britain

Each year, usually on a Sunday in September, ramblers hold a Forbidden Britain Day, keeping up a tradition that dates back to the mass trespass of Kinder Scout moor in April 1932. Small groups all over the country organise protest rallies, walks, meetings and demonstrations in a Right to Roam Freely in Open Countryside campaign. Each individual group decides for itself the form the activity will take, backed by national publicity from the Ramblers' Association and the Open Spaces Society. Look carefully, it might get a column inch in your newspaper or 15 seconds on the local TV news. In southern England this challenge to the local landowners may involve gaining access to enclosed woodland, re-establishing a ploughed-up path, removing barbed wire blocking a right of way or reclaiming some enclosed common land.

In the south the landowners' obsession with blood sports, especially the shooting of pheasant and partridge, has, it is true, preserved some of the traditional features of the landscape such as hedgerows, woods, ponds, streams and commons from the horrors of factory farming. But it has been achieved in the past by denying the poor the land they needed for producing food, and now, with overproduction, by denying everyone recreational access. All so that each year 10 million young pheasants hatched in incubators and reared in sheds can be released to be shot at for fun by a privileged and wealthy few.

In the north of England, Wales and much of Scotland the Day's emphasis is likely to be on a claim for access, to the high uncultivated land usually covered in heather and known to everyone as moorland, which is presently denied, to land which is used for the lucrative rearing and shooting of grouse, not primarily for food but for the sport of killing for the sake of killing. This will bring walkers, formally at least, into conflict with a rather peculiar organisation, the Moorland Association. This is a recently formed private interest group of less than 200 people who are owners of vast areas of Britain, including one third of all English common land. They are campaigning to be able to restrict walkers to the limited number of public footpaths that cross their land. In the North York Moors National Park (a grouse moor owners' stronghold) they have been pressurising the Park Committee to abandon its present policy of open access and, needless to say, their national lobbying seems readily to catch the ear of government ministers.

These landowners would have us believe that we are in their debt for the work they do in conserving the moorland ecology and protecting wild life. Good management, they claim, requires that the moors be protected from human predation. But the truth is leaking out. Far from conserving wild life they destroy any that might prey on their grouse. The secretary of the Moorland Gamekeepers Association has described how fox earths are blocked up with cubs inside so that the addition of a little cyanide creates a perfect gas chamber. The nests of birds of prey, including the hen harrier, one of Britain's rarest, are deliberately trampled on. The Earl of Dalkeith, who has been a leading member of the Nature Conservancy Council, and whose family owns large estates in Scotland, has been praised as a progressive landowner, but one of his former keepers has claimed to have been paid to poison hundreds of birds including owls, sparrow hawks and even rare eagles, or lose his job (*Guardian* 17th August 1990).

In Scotland, whole forests, grouse moors and even mountain ranges may be under single private ownership. The Scots Law of trespass does not deny the right to walk freely across open country but on the other hand it does not protect it. Large areas are increasingly being bought up by financial institutions and wealthy business men as investments. High fences are appearing, sometimes electrified, with boundaries infested with

"Private – Keep Out" notices. Even the native landowners are increasingly trying to keep for themselves and their friends land that has been walked over freely for generations. On one estate on the Isle of Arran the owner proposed to charge geology students £4 a week to examine rock outcrops and was prepared to send out roving parties of gillies (1. Highland Chief's attendant. 2. Man or boy attending sportsmen in Scotland) to catch those who had not paid. Will it be bird watchers, rock climbers and hill walkers next?

So, on next Forbidden Britain Day, give an occasional thought to those who will be trying to reclaim the land for the people and recall the words of Ewan MacColl

"No man has the right to own mountains
Any more than the deep ocean bed."

4

The Battle of Kinder Scout

Kinder Scout, a high plateau of bleak moorland with the Pennine Way passing close to its highest point, is only about 16 miles from both Manchester and Sheffield. Until 1830 it was land open to all and the local villagers used to forage there for whatever it could offer. In 1830 came the enclosure with ownership allotted to the owners of adjoining land and the poor lost their unrestricted rights of access. Now it is visited by 600,000 people a year, the 4,000 acres at the heart of the area are owned by the National Trust and over 76 square miles of the surrounding moorland is subject to access agreements between the Peak National Park Planning Board and the landowners, allowing public access except for up to 12 days a year on which the landowners shoot their grouse.

In the long campaign for access the most dramatic event, which occurred on 24th April 1932, has become part of the mythology of the people's struggle against oppression. Known as the Battle of Kinder Scout, it was awarded its own TV documentary in 1970 and certainly deserves a mention alongside such major events as the Cable Street battle against Mosley's fascists in London's East End in 1936. In comparison, it was quite a small affair involving no more than 600 people, with only six arrests and five subsequent prison sentences, the longest being six months. It is now seen as a landmark in the campaign for access with the story more myth than history, but that is not how it appeared at the time.

The British Workers Sports Federation (BWSF), a Communist Party front organisation which had campaigned successfully for football pitches in deprived areas of London, had begun to organise youth camps in the north. When some of the young workers at such a camp in the village of Rowarth were turned off the moors by gamekeepers the idea of a mass trespass was developed and publicised, in the local press, with leaflets given out at local railway stations and in pubs, and by chalking the pavements. On the day, several hundred people with the usual police escort set off from the recreation ground in the village of Hayfield, the chosen starting point on the Manchester side, and began walking towards William Clough, a narrow valley, with the intention of reaching the summit of Kinder Scout at just over 2000 feet. A few of the crowd left the path, crossed a stream and started up the valley side on their right, where they were challenged by eight gamekeepers armed with sticks. Words were exchanged and a brief fight broke out in which little more than a few bruises were acquired by either side. According to the myth, the crowd then surged to the summit where a victory rally was held. Reality as recorded by several independent eye witness accounts was different. The crowd actually continued along the path to its highest point at Ashop Head and that is where the rally was held, over two miles north west of and 400 feet below the summit. Ironically, except for the brief digression described above, the whole event took place entirely on Snake Path, linking Hayfield with the Snake Inn on the Glossop – Sheffield road, an ancient right of way which had been re-established in 1897 after some 20 years of campaigning by a pioneer group of walkers. The BWSF which orchestrated the mass trespass had not previously been involved in the right-of-access campaign nor did it take any part later. Its leaders did not even know where the summit was and one of them still insists it was reached. The aim of the BWSF was to manipu-

THE BATTLE OF KINDER SCOUT

late a spontaneous protest for its own political ends.

No credit either to the Federation of Rambling Clubs who remained aloof, fearful that the demonstration was more concerned with the class struggle than the access struggle; or to the Commons, Open Spaces and Footpaths Preservation Society which denounced mass trespasses and was in favour of making any kind of trespass a criminal offence. But credit to the ordinary walkers, mainly from local rambling clubs, who saw the need to back up speeches and rallies with a little direct action if the access campaign was going to get anywhere. Credit also to people like George Neale, now in his eighties and living in south London, who happened to be staying in Matlock at the time. Having read about the proposed assault he, with his sister, went to Edale and joined a group of walkers from Sheffield who were approaching Kinder Scout from that side. There was a confrontation with gamekeepers here as well and no-one reached the top. George told me he made his own political statement a week later, when he walked to the summit alone, meeting neither gamekeepers nor police. The authorities had achieved their immediate aims and when the court cases came up there were all the distortions of the truth with which we are familiar today. The size of the crowd was minimised, the violence of the crowd greatly exaggerated and accounts of vicious attacks on gamekeepers invented. An almost entirely peaceful crowd became a gang of hooligans engaged in a general riot. There were those who, at the time, said the trespass contributed nothing to the access campaign, even putting it back 20 years, because it hindered discussion and negotiation; just as earlier there were those who claimed the suffragette activists were irrelevant to the campaign for votes for women; and recently that the defeat of the poll tax owed nothing to the 1990 battle of Trafalgar Square.

With still only half the Peak District National Park's moorland open to the public and access to the adjacent Thurlstone Moor, owned by Yorkshire Water, severely restricted, whatever happened on that day is now recognised as a significant landmark in the continuing campaign for access. A plaque fastened to the rockface of the old quarry near Hayfield commemorates the event and in the 60th anniversary year, Sunday 26th April 1992 was chosen for an "Anniversary Tribute to the Kinder Scout heroes".

In a series of walks across the moors, 500 or so survival-clad walkers converged on Hayfield for a grand procession to nearby Hayfield quarry, now a car park. Here they enjoyed displays and exhibitions to the music of a brass band. There were speeches by Benny Rothman (a veteran of that day) rights of access campaigners and capitalising politicians. In a grand finale, Peggy Seeger, widow of Ewan MacColl, led the congregation with voice and concertina in the 'Manchester Rambler', the song Ewan had written as a young man so many years ago to express his feelings as one of the walkers on that fateful day.

5

Rules or laws?

Critics of anarchism often point to the disorder they consider would result from the abolition of laws. They assume lawlessness equals chaos, talking for example of the mayhem that would ensue if people could please themselves on which side of the road they drove. An inability to distinguish between laws and rules is a characteristic of all those on left or right who believe that a centralised state with the means to enforce the regulations it promulgates is essential if we are to avoid communal castastrophe. Anarchists are always having to explain that people are willing and able to behave according to mutually agreed rules without benefit or need of external coercion. Examples of such self-regulating groups abound even within existing society and include clubs, community associations, co-operatives and squats. They do not have to be small nor geographically confined and many such are described by Colin Ward in *Anarchy in Action*.

A week's walking in the Lake District reminded me that serious fell walkers also constitute such an effective self-regulating group whilst enjoying the freedom of the open air. It is rare to observe behaviour damaging to the environment although the walker is often solitary and unsupervised. They are invariably adequately equipped and protected against the notoriously changeable weather.

No litter is left, gates are closed, walls are neither climbed nor damaged, paths are followed, dogs kept on leads and, in the lambing season, are more likely to be left at home. Cairns are preserved or added to and are invaluable aids in keeping to the path in mist or low cloud.

Fell walkers come from all over the country for short periods at a time and share the environment with sheep farmers who depend on this land for a living. There is a real possibility of tension between the two groups yet they coexist amicably and on occasion are mutually supportive. The walker will tell the farmer of sheep he has seen in trouble and, more seriously, in the event of an accident a voluntary Mountain Rescue Team of very experienced local walkers and climbers will turn out. Many of these are likely to be farmers. Both groups behave responsibly with a mutual interest in avoiding damage to and pollution of the environment.

Attention has been drawn to the need to marry freedom of the fells with responsibility particularly with reference to the problem of path erosion. This is seen at its worst in Derbyshire at the southern end of the Pennine Way and on parts of the three popular peaks of the Yorkshire Dales, Penyghent, Ingleborough and Whernside. Some pessimists talk of closing National Parks at busiest times or having access regulated by ticket quotas. Yet even in August, when the lakeland roads are one continuous traffic jam, the higher fells are comparatively empty. More positively some clubs are voluntarily foregoing use of the most popular paths for a time, to allow for natural regeneration. In the Lake District the natural stone which abounds is being used to remake the most eroded paths. The product, several feet wide, blends readily into the environment yet is clearly visible and easy to follow. This gives the land on each side time to recover. *Country Walking* magazine in its May 1990 issue described the work of a team of four experts plus volunteers who repaired the ancient packhorse route over Sty Head pass in Bòrrowdale, using the traditional method of 'pitching'. This involves laying stones in a trench flat face downwards and infilling with soil so that grass soon covers a hard stone base. When completed the work is hardly visible but can withstand the wear and tear of walkers' boots.

The day-to-day work of maintaining much of the Lake District environment is mainly in the hands of the National Trust. As a national organisation the policies of the Trust reflect its largely bourgeois middle-class membership and are rarely likely to appeal to libertarians let alone anarchists. However the work carried out on the ground by the wardens of the National Park with the help of volunteers and, it must be said, MSC/ET labour is to be welcomed. The maintenance of paths, stiles and bridges is carried out with enthusiasm and dedication. This, together with the assistance and advice they are ready to give to visitors, helps to ensure that the high fells continue to be available to all, for the peaceful enjoyment of walking and climbing.

6

A Catnap on Catbells

Sitting on the summit of Catbells in the Lake District, 1500 feet above sea level, sharing my cheese sandwich with a persistent sheep, I pondered on the conflict of interests between sheep farmers and fell walkers. Back in London with the reference books I looked for evidence that fell walking was a nuisance to the upland sheep farmers of northern England, but found none. True that at a conference on moorlands management and access held in 1979 a land agent did claim that unrestricted access to the North Yorkshire Moors would force sheep farmers to leave, but as he was from Blenheim Palace near Oxford it was hardly the voice of experience talking.

Sheep farming has flourished alongside tourism in the Lakes and North Wales for many years and although some farmers claim that ramblers disturb hill-grazing sheep, the evidence is against them. A study carried out by the University of Newcastle upon Tyne in 1976 on The Impact of Recreation on Upland Access Land could find little evidence of damage to sheep rearing caused by walkers. Typically, Kinder Scout moor, crossed by the Pennine Way which is walked by thousands each year, now carries three times as many sheep as in pre-access days and this is due almost entirely to an increase in grazing density.

Dogs are another matter and sheep-worrying is a menace especially during the lambing season, but anyone who has walked with a club will have been made aware of the concern there is that dogs are kept under proper control, indeed many clubs will not agree to members bringing dogs on to sheep-rearing hills.

Erosion is increasing on these grassed uplands and walkers are often blamed for this but in 1981 the Peak Park Board published a study of the problem under the title Moorland Erosion Study Phase I Report. This concluded that as a cause of erosion walkers came way down the list, after partial loss of vegetation due to more periods of drier weather and, especially, pollution with heavy metals and sulphur dioxide from the surrounding industrial areas which kill mosses and lichens. The collapse of northern manufacturing industry will now, ironically, benefit the hills.

The 64,000 hill farmers of Britain are, it is true, in serious trouble but it is not from walkers. As farmers of marginal land suitable for little except sheep rearing they depend on subsidies to survive. Indeed, their needs have been used by the National Farmers' Union to extract ever larger grants which then go as much to the well off lowland farmers as to those who really need them. Faced now with drastic cuts in subsidies and increased competition from some lowland farmers who met falling cereal prices by partially switching to sheep rearing, the hill farmers are again in trouble and reduced to lobbying an indifferent government. The French farmers are none too pleased either. Take the sheep off the hills and they would be covered with impenetrable scrub within a few years and a unique environment would be destroyed; a loss of pleasure for the hill walker but a loss of livelihood for the hill farmer.

Let us as walkers give the hill farmers our support and join with them to save the hills whilst condemning the factory farming plutocrats of middle and eastern England.

7

Rutland or Orwell land

The Viking Way is a long-distance footpath from the Humber Bridge, through the Lincolnshire Wolds, around the edge of the Fens to the Vale of Belvoir: 120 miles of ordinary but not dull walking. Having none of the excitement and popularity of the more famous Pennine Way, it is little used but is ideal for the elderly and the not so firm. The final section is in Rutland, the ancient but now non-existent English county that refuses to be absorbed into the 20th century.

Rutland conjures up a picture of pastoral bliss, medieval merry England, bucolic labourers and landed gentry, but it is just the eastern part of a Leicestershire which doesn't welcome walkers. Although, according to the map, it is criss-crossed by footpaths it was recently described by the Chair of the Ramblers' Association as bandit country for innocent walkers of Rights of Way. One third of the paths cross land made unwalkable by farmers each year and a recent survey showed that in this part of England half the paths were poor or unusable and there was only a 60 per cent chance of completing a two-mile country walk.

The feeling of being under constant surveillance reminiscent of Orwell's 1984 is not what one would expect in such a rural environment yet in just two days' walking, and after declining to take coffee with Lady Tollemache of Buckminster, we were challenged by a man with a gun, accosted by three men on horseback, almost scalped by military aircraft, monitored with binoculars by two men in a jeep, chased by an angry farmer on a tractor and goggled at by a crowd of excited Italian men who almost completely filled Wymondham's small country pub. But let me explain.

Within a mile of the start of our walk, near the pleasant village of Sewstern, an abrupt challenge by a young man with a gun who appeared from the proverbial thicket made us think that we had strayed into a secret nuclear establishment or a regional seat of government. But no, we had only strayed from the permitted path, it was private land and we were disturbing the game birds. Back on the Viking Way we met three fox hunters who had not only lost the fox, but the dogs, the other horses and their riders as well. We could not help them but did say what we thought of their sporting activities. Shortly after, we had to cross the northern perimeter of Cottesmore airfield as sinister black war planes repetitively took off, circled and landed. The pilots were clearly beginners and it was difficult to avoid ducking each time one passed over. The control tower in the distance stood out above the flat landscape and you had the feeling that drifting a foot from the path would quickly put you in the guardroom.

It was a relief to escape from the airfield towards the quiet village of Exton on the edge of, or is it in, the estate of the Rt. Hon. the 5th Earl of Gainsborough (recreations shooting and sailing). The path passing through agricultural and parkland was clearly marked if only because every conceivable deviation is signposted 'Private – Keep Out'. These fields are lower than the surrounding land, the result of ancient ironstone quarrying, and on nearby higher ground we could see a stationary jeep and the occupants could see us. We met them later.

So, into Exton and the village pub, which was busy feeding a coach load of pensioners. We were able to eat in the rear garden once mine host had unlocked the fire exit. Because of the high wall we could only catch an occasional glimpse of the attractive-looking park and a native explained that it was very private, but recommended the local church for its collection of interesting tombs. Disappointed, we skirted the high wall until we reached a small door near a group of council houses. It was not locked, so dare we go in? Of course you can said the tenants, Catholics are allowed into the park to attend Lord Gainsborough's Catholic church attached to the big house (and incidentally to enjoy the park). So we did, if a trifle furtively, in case our atheism was showing.

Leaving Exton on our return journey, we again took a wrong turning, but within minutes the two men in that jeep had arrived to courteously shepherd us back to the correct path.

That only leaves the man on a tractor and the Italians. The farmer was angry because with our map and compass he thought we were from the Ramblers' Association and were trying to establish a new right of way across his land. And the Italians? Well, the publican said "Oh, they often eat here". I leave the explanation to your imagination.

8

Don't Covet Prince's Covert

The problems you meet walking in Surrey differ sharply from those of the high open moors, as sharply as the scenery itself. They are mostly small-scale irritants such as having to deal with a yard high load of manure dumped in front of a stile when there is no way round or, rather more mischievously, when barbed wire is stapled to the underside of the wooden top hand board of a stile with just enough showing to do real damage. Occasionally, however, they can be quite bizarre.

There is a particular piece of woodland in Surrey, nothing special, even a little scruffy, which is apparently managed in a half-hearted way for the wood it yields and possibly used for the occasional shoot. At one entrance a handsome lodge stands guard over a padlocked gate whilst at another there is only a sign to let you know that this is not common land you are entering. You can walk through it but you have to get permission first.

To get permission you have to write to the Queen, well, not exactly the Queen because royalty does not directly handle such menial administrative matters, so you write to the Crown Estates Office. Even they will not answer your letter themselves, but in a less well known example of privatisation, or should it be commonisation, they will pass it to a firm of chartered surveyors who will write to you asking for more information. Not, so far as I know, how you voted or didn't vote at the last election, but why, what day, what time do you wish to walk through this wood, how many of you will there be and which paths will you take? Here is a map, please mark out your precise route and return it to us, we will then consider your request.

Permission was granted with a promise to unlock the gate but of course there were conditions. No responsibility would be accepted for any misfortune that might befall any member of the party, and on the other hand the party would be held strictly liable for any damage that might be caused, however inadvertently. Get out of that if you can.

We did walk the mile or so across this partly culled woodland and, except for a cheery chap sitting in his makeshift shelter eating his sandwiches who gave us a friendly wave, we saw no-one. We left the wood through the gate which had been left unlocked as promised, although it would have been easier to climb over it than over some of the stiles thoughtfully provided by farmers.

We didn't think the helicopter which passed overhead was there to keep an eye on this small group of elderly ramblers but you never can tell. Neither did we think we had crossed a potential site of monarchal government by decree should opposition to the poll tax have caused a breakdown in the bureaucratic fabric of society. So why did we bother to walk this particular path? Because it links two established Rights of Way but you cannot have a right of way across crown land. It probably once was, but would it be again should ownership change?

There was apparently a plan to sell the land (times can be hard even for the rich). This involved a proposal to develop the site with a five star hotel and conference centre and some houses, shops and offices. But surely you cannot do that in green belt Surrey? Yes, you can, because that was only the small print and the large print described a plan to build a massive sports and leisure centre; and that's all right in a green belt even if most of us would not be able to afford to use it. That was some years ago and the plan fell through for lack of sufficient capital. However, rumour has it that someone may try again. So, if anyone comes round wanting to borrow the odd million, don't let them have it – even for a good cause like a sports and leisure centre in Prince's Covert. A mass trespass might stop such a plan, but who wants to be locked up in the Tower of London for High Treason?

9

An expensive path

You could be shot for it, accidentally of course, the greatest crime of all, disturbing the game birds. More commonly it will just be expensive, which is what happened in Wychwood Forest, part of the Oxfordshire 2,500 acre estate of the Rt. Hon. Lord Rotherwick, as he likes to be called. Here, every year, up to 10,000 pheasants, 180 deer and 50 ducks are shot by his paying guests. He clearly does not much like his neighbours, for an ancient footpath running for a mile and a quarter through the woods has been closed to the public for 24 years. Local villagers were allowed to collect firewood on two mornings a week and we could all walk along one of his paths on one day of the year, Palm Sunday as it happens.

At least, that was the situation, but in 1985 the Conservatives lost control of Oxfordshire County Council and the new council began helping walkers' and community group attempts to get the path reopened, recognising that it would provide a useful link in the local pathway network. Although he hosts the West Oxfordshire Conservatives' annual jamboree on his estate, the good lord said No, it would interfere with all the killing for pleasure I provide. I would also lose my privacy; Cornbury House where I live, when I am not staying in my mews flat in S.W.1, is only 800 yards from the path. It is true that he would not be able to see the walkers from his house, but as his land agent said "Lord Rotherwick would know they were there".

Rotherwick found an expert who calculated he would lose about £45,000 a year, made up of £29,200 for the shooting of fewer pheasants and deer, £5,000 for the increased deer damage to crops and trees and the cost of preventing it, and £10,000 for an extra gamekeeper to guard against poaching. He calculated compensation for his losses at £600,000.

A long campaign culminated, as is usual in these matters, in a public inquiry presided over by an inspector. He announced his decision in December 1988 with the comment "the proposed path will add considerably to the convenience and enjoyment of a substantial section of the public and persons resident in the area and it is expedient that the path should be created".

The path is now open and that should have been the end of the matter, but Rotherwick thought otherwise. He valued his estate at £11 million (well, house prices had risen) and demanded £1.6 million in compensation from the council. This, as John Vidal pointed out in *The Guardian*, worked out at £713 a yard or £20 an inch. But, as a Conservative councillor said "who wants a footpath through their garden? Be it kitchen garden or a forest, you are entitled to compensation."

10

Our Forbidden Land

For a change let's look at a book of pictures, pictures of the countryside, but with a difference. Fay Godwin, probably Britain's foremost landscape photographer, has produced in her recent book *Our Forbidden Land* (Jonathan Cape, p/b £12.95), as a contribution to her three years as President of the Ramblers' Association, a collection of black and white photographs that tell the story of a land desecrated by industrial, agricultural and military vandals interspersed with scenes of unspoiled beauty. Here is Stonehenge in all its mystery, but seen through barbed wire; the Avebury circle, in danger of becoming just another side show in a theme park; and Faslane submarine base, seen through layers of high wire fencing that would tax the ingenuity of any peace activist to penetrate, is contrasted with the domesticity of Faslane Peace Camp.

And of course there are the notices that now litter the countryside. No climbing, no camping, no hill walking, no admittance, no access, no entry, no this, no that, but not no fucking for this is land owned by gentlemen, concerned for the proprieties. North West Water may be proud of their "This is your drinking water NO ADMITTANCE" but they should have added "Unless you want to build a theme park or a time-share estate" for did they not advertise for a manager to develop their landholdings commercially? Not all the notices are prohibitive, some offer friendly information such as "Dogs shot".

On the positive side this is also a book of photographs that convey the beauty of the countryside and contrasting landscapes through the seasons, which gains by being in black and white.

Her previous books have also been a celebration of the countryside but this one, which must be her best so far, comes with a harder edge. There are brief accounts of the successes and failures in recent years in the campaign for free access to uncultivated land but her 30,000 word accompanying text is primarily a magnificently sustained personal polemic against agrichemical business, modern farming methods, the military, the nuclear power industry, road transport policies, the Official Secrets Act, politicians, governments and those landowners trying to deny us access to the North English Moors, yes, you've guessed it, the Moorland Association.

She attacks the Ministry of Agriculture, Fisheries and Food (MAFF) in particular for its role in introducing Bovine Spongiform Encephalitis to our dinner plates and genetically engineered hormone Bovine Somatotrophin into our milk. And did you know that MAFF protects the interests of the factory farmers by imposing the same Salmonella inspection fee whether you have 25 hens or 25,000, putting real free range eggs out of the reach of most town dwellers?

You may not accept her solutions but you can enjoy her argument against "government agencies who seem to think they can censor as well as try to copyright the landscape of our heritage". English Heritage tried to charge her £200 per visit to photograph Stonehenge whilst trying not to get entangled with a crew making an advertising film, and the Ministry of Works with their red tape interrogations interfered with her photography of Avebury.

The book is not organised into chapters, but themes are subtly introduced and include Pathways through history, Learning to love the environment, Theft, MOD remains, The National Trust and the military, Inner city space; so you are not too surprised when turning a page to move from a derelict military urinal to a stone lion at Chatsworth.

Menwith Hill

Photo John Brierly

Menwith Hill

Photo Paula Solloway

NOTICE

PRIVATE MOORLAND TRESPASSING PROHIBITED

Forbidden Britain Day – Mickle Fell Co. Durham

Photo Ramblers' Association

Forbidden Britain Day – Ploughed out path near Ladbroke. Photo Ramblers' Association

Forbidden Britain Day – Shirburn & Pyrton Hills

Photo Rambler's Association

Forbidden Britain Day – Hannifield Reservoir Point of Trespass

Photo Ramblers' Association

Footpath sign under water

Photo Fay Godwin

Greenham Common *Photo Fay Godwin*

Some news is good, as for instance that which makes me want to visit Dean Clough in Halifax to see what has replaced the defunct Crossley Carpet Mills. Variety is introduced with excerpts from Crouch and Ward's book *The Allotment* and Rendell and Ward's book *Undermining the Central Line* and poems by Peggy Seeger, Ewan MacColl, Adrian Mitchell, Stevie Smith and many others. There is also an excellent bibliography.

This is a book to be dipped into again and again. It is available from large bookshops, but don't expect to find it in the Politics or Environment sections. Such is the idiosyncracy of booksellers that you had better look in the photography section, where it may well be between books on how to use an SLR and how to take the most exciting glamour pictures.

Incidentally, what do you do if you unintentionally get caught in cross-fire on Dartmoor? Godwin describes Chris Brasher using his mobile phone to get them to stop shooting. I guess you and I would just have to run like hell.

11

In the firing line

Not much chance of being shot at on a country walk in Southern England, you might think, yet on a recent walk through Redlands Wood in Surrey we did feel at risk. The path gradually narrowed, finally ending in impenetrable bramble beneath which we found the remains of a wooden notice board lying face down on the ground. We deciphered its message to read "DANGER rifle range" and a glance at the O.S. map later confirmed this. We did not linger, nor search for victims in the undergrowth.

Further north they arrange things differently. In the Peak District National Park, access agreements allow landowners to close the moors to walkers for up to 12 shooting days a year, provided these are publicised well in advance. This protects innocent walkers and the grouse unfortunately cannot read. In 1990 however, for fear that saboteurs would interfere with their pleasure, they decided to keep their shooting days secret and the walker would take his or her chance along with the grouse. Then they had a better idea, to persuade the Peak Park Board to close the moors altogether in August, except of course for the sportsmen, claiming that there was a fire risk. That would keep out both walkers and saboteurs. The public protested and the ban was lifted.

Of course the main danger to walkers in the National Parks often comes from the MOD who insist on using land in the parks for live firing practice with their tanks and artillery; they also claim to be protecting rare plant species. Exactly how much land they are using is not disclosed but it includes 15 per cent of Dartmoor and 22 per cent of the Northumberland parks as well as some of the Peak District and the Pembrokeshire Coast.

A study by Dr. Susan Owens published in 1990 entitled 'Military Live Firing in National Parks' had been commissioned from the U.K. Centre for Economic and Environmental Development by the Council for National Parks, Council for Protection of Rural England, Dartmoor Preservation Association, Open Spaces Society and Ramblers' Association. It concluded, perhaps not surprisingly, that the military were using too much land for live firing and should give up some of it, starting with land they used in National Parks. It also suggested that they should pay for what they still used and their claimed needs be subject to public scrutiny. Chris Patten then Environment Secretary, even less surprisingly did not see things that way at all and promptly proceeded to approve an MOD application to rebuild Willsworthy Barracks in Dartmoor National Park to house soldiers using, for their war games, land on licence from the Duchy of Cornwall. So their landlord is the environmentally conscious conservationist Charles who promised in 1985 to consider seriously whether live firing should be allowed to continue when the licence came up for renewal in 1991. Promises, promises; the MOD not only got its licence renewed, but this time for another 21 years.

This is all going to get worse now the British army of the Rhine is not going to have the North German plain to practise on and the tanks and fifty thousand troops have to be accommodated at home. The MOD has been quietly buying up another 50,000 acres and may have its eyes on your favourite open space. We can expect to see many more signs saying "Battle area, no access" like the one on Thetford Heath. Perhaps they should be put in a Middle East desert, but that would be unfair to the Bedouins.

And have you heard about the German village of Fibua in the Wiltshire countryside? The Germans refused to have it and the proposed site here was moved 200 yards across a local council boundary so that planning permission could be obtained without a public enquiry. FIBUA stands for "Fighting in Built Up Areas" and that is just what the army use it for, and no prizes for guessing why they need it. The villagers of nearby Chitterne are very upset about the noise.

Finally, not a matter of live firing but an assault on the senses and a desecration of the countryside to boot. Soldiers (officers really) of the King's Own Border Regiment proposed to use stones to mark out on the ground a giant replica (195 feet by 130 feet) of their regimental badge, and this on a wild, open stretch of common land overlooking the M6 motorway near the Lake District. The idea was approved with acclaim by the local Tebay Parish Council. This is not surprising as the good burghers of Tebay have been happy over the years to keep unemployment down by encouraging the local lads to join the regiment and have no doubt subscribed generously towards a new war memorial whenever needed. However the regiment had to abandon its plan because of public protests: or was it because they realised how easily a few comrades could have rearranged the stones one night to create an enormous letter A?

12

Walking in Waterland

If you bought shares in one of the water companies at the end of 1989 and later sold them, you were then no doubt able to share with your stockbroker the profit you made. I believe some people bought a few shares so that they could take a protesting voice to future annual general meetings. More likely you had nothing to do with the whole sordid business, seeing it as just another way the government has found to transfer money from the poor to the rich.

Leaving aside for the time being the effect this will have on us as consumers of water in terms of its future quality and cost, consider the water authorities (should we now call them companies?) as major landowners. In the Peak District National Park, three water authorities own 80 square miles, which is 15% of the total 542 square miles of the park. Altogether some 750 square miles are involved, much of it open upland moorland. This is land which nominally at least belonged to all of us, most of it freely available for recreational walking but which is now privately owned. Can this land be developed? Might we find our path blocked by a chemical factory, a luxury time-share hotel development, a massive tourist leisure complex complete with undercover tropical rainforest? Or perhaps we will just have to pay to walk where previously we could roam freely, with turnstiles to negotiate and ticket collectors to restrict us? Will the fire services, who now draw water freely from the reservoirs to deal with summer fires, find the water is metered, with the bill to follow later? Water authorities are already instructing staff to pursue commercial initiatives.

Commercial companies have a duty to their shareholders to be economic and efficient, euphemisms for maximising profits, and it is clear that the government originally intended that the water companies should be free to use or dispose of the land as they chose. Pressure from interested groups did modify this slightly.

In 20% of water authority land, mostly in the Lake District, an attempt was made to cancel an existing legal right to roam but was abandoned. For the rest of these acres the privatised water undertakings are required to have regard to the desirability of preserving for the public any freedom of access. No doubt they will think about it, all the way to the bank. The water companies are not free to sell land unless the Secretary of State approves and conditions may be imposed. These are the kinds of detail determined by parliamentary bills and debated by our politicians. But who reads Hansard? And who would trust a Secretary of State?

The three quarters of a million hill walkers are not going to give up their right to walk this land, and to do so without making any payment. In May 1989 over 3000 people attended a meeting at Rivington in Lancashire at which one of the speakers was 77 year old Benny Rothman, a leader of the famous mass trespass of Kinder Scout in 1932. They pledged to exercise their traditional right of access to the hills by continuing to walk on the half a million acres of water authority land after privatisation and not to be deterred by the threat of legal action for trespass. One of the unexpected offshoots of privatisation could therefore be the biggest confrontation seen in the countryside since 1932. They have been warned.

13

Pesticides with everything

When seeds specially selected to produce high yielding crops turn out to be more susceptible to pests, the agrochemical industry obligingly produces toxic chemicals to deal with the problem. We learn to live with the side effects, consuming our sub-lethal doses of these chemicals with our food. Take a walk in the country and you may have the pleasure of being showered with them as well. Some of the £450 million a year (1986 figure) spent on pesticides and sprayed from the high-tech machines now ubiquitous on large farms may fall on footpaths and, if you happen to be passing, on you. Some farmers stop spraying whilst you pass, others don't notice or don't care. The use of aerial spraying is also increasing, so if you see a low flying aircraft approaching, take cover if you can and wish you had a gas mask. One chemist in the pesticide industry has claimed "almost no pesticide or herbicide in use today should present a hazard to anyone walking through a sprayed crop – unless they rolled naked in it immediately after spraying". So, do be careful where you take off your clothes. However, even clothed, some walkers have suffered headaches, nausea and worse after getting too close to a shower of pesticide.

Remember DDT? In general use 30 years ago and a very effective pest killer it was. But it was also damaging to wildlife, particularly birds and insects, and became concentrated in the food chain. Most of us probably still have detectable amounts of DDT in our fatty tissues although it has not been used in this country since 1984. Government chemists began to suspect it of disturbing hormonal balance in humans and, whether because of this or the public outcry about its effects on the environment, its use was discontinued. However Swedish scientists, by analysing pine needles of different ages from across Europe, have demonstrated that air contaminated with DDT drifted into Western Europe from East Germany in 1984 and suggest that it was still being used then in Eastern Europe.

Grain destined for storage is sprayed with pesticide by agricultural workers to protect it from attack by insects. It has been shown recently that when such grain is fed experimentally to laboratory rats and mice, sufficient pesticide is absorbed to cause mild liver damage. These results suggest that what is now officially accepted as a safe level of pesticide contamination is not so safe and provides more evidence of the excessive use of chemicals in farming.

New chemicals are continually being marketed and there are arguments about the dangers they present, but there is no disagreement that the facilities for independent checking of their safety are inadequate. In 1989, unions, Friends of the Earth and other conservation groups were joined bizarrely by the British Agrochemicals Association in a demand for more and better checking of the safety of pesticides. Most of this work is at present done by about 40 government scientists working at the Ministry of Agriculture laboratory at Harpenden near London and toxicity details are, of course, secret. They are in the process of reviewing the 120 pesticides already in use and checking up to 40 new ones produced each year. As a result only a few of these are approved annually and it has been claimed that at present rates it would take 40 years to clear the backlog. Now you can see that the concern of the agrochemical industry is not so bizarre after all. A five-year campaign, to make the data on safety more widely available did achieve some success, when in November 1991 MAAF announced that consumer groups would be allowed to nominate their own expert representative on the Advisory Committee on Pesticides and that safety data on pesticides approved before 1986 would be made public.

We are exposed to some risks from the agricultural use of pesticides due to the greed and stupidity of some farmers and the profit-seeking efforts of industry, but according to the *Southern Resister* something much more sinister has gone on at the Boscombe Down air base on the edge of Salisbury Plain. In addition to its recent use as a Cruise missile base and as a base for F-111 bombers it harboured a couple of old Hawker Hunters which were used to spray toxic substances on to troops doing chemical warfare training on the nearby Porton ranges. Of course sometimes things go wrong. A few years ago they missed the troops and sprayed herbicide on adjacent farmland. In October 1989 one of the planes, in trouble, ditched its unidentified chemical load in mid-air and Amesbury was at the receiving end. The visible damage was paint stripped from cars but who knows or cares about the harm that might have been done to the people who, unlike the soldiers, had no protective clothing. Of course it took some time and pressure before the Ministry of Defence would admit that it was not an attack by aliens from outer space.

14

Taking the lid off Lydd

Some stories, like this one, eventually have a happy ending, and like all good stories, it has a moral. If you break a law the state will punish you, unless of course you are the state. You have heard the moral before, no doubt, but perhaps you have not heard the story.

There is an army training ground near Lydd in Kent and there are public footpaths across it, but for some years the public could not walk on them because fencing kept them out. A few years ago the Ramblers' Association finally got so upset about this that they wrote to Richard Hatfield, Head of Defence Lands, complaining, and he replied that the MOD respected existing rights of way. So that was all right then, and a chat with the training area commandant at Lydd should have sorted things out. But when approached he was reported to have said "We are not able to permit access to the routes followed by rights of way which were in effect closed some nine years ago." So, no law has been broken because the paths are still there, you just cannot use them. Orwell would have approved. However such a fuss was made about this that Roger Freeman, then Armed Forces Minister, issued a statement promising to open the blocked paths. It couldn't be that easy, could it? And it wasn't; Kent County Council, without any local consultation, stated that it intended to extinguish and divert the said paths. However its ignominious conniving with the army failed and the footpaths across Romney Marshes linking Lydd with the sea cannot now be closed.

Lord Justice Woolf, sitting with Mr. Justice Pill, in the Queen's Bench Divisional Court, ruled that Kent County Council had not carried out correctly the Statutory Procedures laid down in the 1980 Highways Act, so reversing a decision made earlier by Folkstone Magistrates. The notice put up by the council stating their intention to block up the paths "misleadingly" stated that there would be an alternative route. Or as a non-legal mind would put it, they lied. The case was brought by the Ramblers' Association and the council had to pay their costs. So the paths the MOD were forced to open will stay open. Sometimes the law games played by the judiciary conflict with the war games played by the military, to the benefit of us walkers. But will the council start the Blocking procedure all over again and will the army continue to use the firing range?

The army occupies vast areas of this land, keeping walkers and farming out of some of our finest countryside and it never seems to have enough. For example 23% of the Northumberland National Park, and 14% of Dartmoor National Park is occupied and the heath and forest of the Suffolk Brecklands are largely inaccessible due to the heavy military presence, yet it has also been after 500 acres near Sherwood Forest and 3000 acres at Little Cressingham in Norfolk. In 1988 it set out to double the size of its training grounds on Holcombe Moor near Manchester by seizing a further 960 acres of public access common land. Despite three years of grass roots opposition, after a public enquiry it was given the go ahead. Ironically, in September 1992 the MOD. decided that it did not feel it would be appropriate to proceed with the proposal. Where will it turn to next and will more footpaths be threatened? And by the way, did you know that there is a public footpath across the USAF base at RAF Lakenheath? But more about that later.

15

Tramping the tarmac

We walked through the main gate along Yarmouth, Norwich and Rochester Roads, with just a passing glance at Donutland, the Burger Bar and the new dormitory project still under construction. With our anoraks and boots we looked like a group of country walkers although it did not look like a country path. But it was a Right of Way and the notice at the gate insisted, under Statutory Instruments 1986 No. 8: Nothing in these byelaws shall affect the lawful exercise by any person of a public right of way.

It was 1st January 1990 and we were walking across United States Air Force base Lakenheath which housed four squadrons of F-111 nuclear bombers and from where on the 15th April 1986 planes flew to bomb Libya. Twenty persons and a dog had joined John Bugg* in the company of two Anglia TV men and a reporter from the Cambridge *Evening News*. We were escorted by five Ministry of Defence police whilst a police vehicle kept at a semi-discreet distance. In ten minutes we had reached a gate in the high perimeter fence which led to what is left of the footpath. The gate, normally locked, was open that day, protected only by two sinister men in a parked truck. For those who approached the base using the footpath a phone is thoughtfully provided so that the key holder and presumably an appropriate escort can be summoned. At least you can do this now that the phone is no longer unhelpfully situated, out of reach inside the fence. After some of us had used it to chat to 'control' about our admiration for our gallant American defenders, we returned, complete with escort to the main gate. There we met some late arrivals, disappointed to have missed the fun, so we did it all over again.

On Sunday 15th April 1990, the fourth anniversary of the Libyan raid, some of us and a different dog joined John Bugg to

---

*John Bugg died on January 31, 1993

repeat the walk to maintain our right to use this "highway" for the purpose of political protest, although this time we did not have the benefit of media coverage. Two protesters carried a banner stating "on this day 1986 USAF Lakenheath bombed the innocents of Tripoli an act of cowardice bringing shame to us all". The Burger Bar seemed to have disappeared (or was it being rebuilt bigger and better?) and the Dormitory Project was nearing completion. Did that mean more Americans were coming?

It is due to a curiosity of our legal system that we were able to amble somewhat ludicrously across a military airfield and the MOD set out to stop such nonsense by getting the path "extinguished", a legal but singularly appropriate term meaning no more walking across our, sorry, this American base. To stop the MOD we had to show that the path, although of no scenic value, was both needed and used and we each had our own reasons for taking this walk. John Bugg concerned at the erosion of our civil liberties and right to roam has regularly walked this path to protest against the killing of Raafat El Ghossein, an 18 year old Libyan in Tripoli, by a bomb dropped from a US F-111 bomber from Lakenheath. We were supporting his right to use a public highway to make a political protest against an act which was carried out with the consent and, indeed, approval of the British government.

The Government, in trouble with its military byelaws, had hoped to persuade Forest Heath District Council to extinguish the path, but between our two visits the Council had received so many letters insisting that it was needed as a short cut, for recreation and for political protest, that it referred the matter back to its Health and Amenities Committee. The result was that the council decided, in spite of protests by its more jingoistic members, to abandon its attempts to stop us walking across the base, rather than face the cost and inconvenience of a public enquiry. To add to the trouble the government has been having with these byelaws, Mildenhall magistrates dismissed a prosecution case for trespass against several peace campaigners on the grounds that the offence was not known in law because the byelaws had not been correctly introduced. Anyone arrested under these byelaws, whether charged or not, could apply pressure for redress by writing to the Lord Chancellor, Home Secretary and Attorney General.

Although the footpath could be extinguished by Statutory Instrument of Parliament it is, at the time of writing, still open,

(John Bugg walked it on 15th February 1992), the telephone is still there and the military still willing and able to provide an escort for your safety. So do keep on walking whenever you can.

16

Greenham Common

When a famous judge, former Master of the Rolls, Lord Denning, stated that the commoners of Greenham had a right to cut the wire that prevented them having access to a large part of one of the finest open spaces in southern England, the world (or that part of it called Greenham Common) might seem to have turned upside down. Had not the Women of Greenham peace camp been cutting the wire since 1981 and, as a result, been regularly arrested, prosecuted and fined or imprisoned?

This area of sandy heathland on a chalk ridge, two miles from the centre of Newbury, was bought by the town council in 1938, with the help of the Open Spaces Society, to preserve it as a public open space. In 1941 it was requisitioned by the government for use as an RAF base and in 1951 handed over to the USAF under wartime defence regulations. These expired in 1958 so that all subsequent military building, fences, aircraft hangers, silos and the recreational facilities, clubs and churches the Americans cannot manage without, have been illegal. But when did that bother the government?

To further complicate matters, Newbury Council, when threatened with a compulsory purchase order in 1960, sold the base to the Air Ministry, although with covenants restricting its disposal when no longer needed as a base. The Open Spaces Society and others campaigning for the return of the common to the public, did in 1973 succeed, with the help of the commoners, in getting the commoners' rights registered, despite obstruction by the Ministry of Defence. However their rights to graze animals, dig for gravel and collect wood were held in abeyance.

From 1981 these efforts were reinforced by the women of the Greenham peace camps, using their own ineffable methods, which provoked the then Secretary of State for Defence, Michael Heseltine no less, to react. In 1985 he invoked the Military Land Act of 1892 to enable him to pass the Greenham Common No Entry Byelaws (1986). Parliament, the supposed guardian of our rights and freedoms, failed to notice that the 1892 Act specifically excluded the right to take away or prejudicially affect any Right of Common. But the women of Greenham did notice and argued in court repetitively that this made the byelaws invalid and therefore their prosecutions for trespassing the base illegal. When two of the women did succeed in persuading Reading Crown Court to quash a conviction for trespass made by Newbury magistrates, this decision was overturned in October 1988 by the High Court and the case returned to the Crown Court with instructions to convict. Judge Schiemann's ruling in this case deserves wide publicity as it shows the tortuous reasoning establishment figures can achieve when wrong-footed by the people. To summarise, I hope accurately, his ruling: Well, yes, commoners cannot have their rights removed under this act, so the byelaws are indeed invalid. But they would have been O.K. if only Michael had remembered to exempt the commoners. Now let's assume the byelaws had exempted commoners from these restrictions, then they would be valid. You two women are not commoners, so hard luck, case dismissed and you may not appeal to the House of Lords. There are ways round this however and the women found one and did appeal to the House of Lords.

Meanwhile the government, faced with the possibility of being unable to stop the Greenham women from walking all over the base, which they indeed were doing during this interim period, and the possibility of claims for compensation for all those wrongful arrests, had to think of something quickly. The important thing was to get rid of these rights of common and, as an MOD spokesman said, that should not be too difficult, after all they cannot graze their sheep because the wire stops them and with central heating they do not need kindling. To try to get rid of them the government adopted the stick and carrot approach. First the carrot. If they all agreed to forfeit their rights to that part of the common which is a built-up USAF base, they would each receive £750. Now for the stick. If they did not all agree by

6 January 1990, the Defence Act of 1854 would be used to abolish these rights. Some of the 60-odd commoners just wanted more money, but three of them refused to accept the deal and were publicly named and vilified in the local press.

When the ultimatum expired the MOD stated that it intended to carry out its threat, as the action to remove commoners' rights was necessary according to a written answer in the House of Commons "to remove a legal obstacle to construction on MOD property". Although the MOD had bought the land, change of ownership does not extinguish the rights of commoners and therefore others to have access and these rights stood in the way of future military use, or sale of the land for private development in another privatisation bonanza. Lord Denning believed the MOD lawyers had got it wrong and that 19th century statutes could not override common law and extinguish commoners' rights. He, together with Richard Adams (author of *Watership Down*) and other notable locals, formed a group called "Commons Again" to campaign for the common to be returned to the people when the Cruise missiles had gone.

Back to the House of Lords and on 12 July 1990 they ruled that the 1985 byelaws, which prohibited entry to the base, infringed Rights of Common and were therefore illegal, and all charges made under them invalid. So the 1986 conviction of the two Greenham women had been overturned and the world of Greenham tilted again. The refusal by some commoners to accept the extinguishing of their rights had been rewarded. The BBC TV news briefly showed the peace camp women celebrating, ITN did not. Instead of the law pursuing the women of Greenham, more than a thousand of them who had been convicted by Newbury magistrates were free to pursue the law with claims for damages and compensation for wrongful arrest and imprisonment, always provided they could surmount the hurdles of misinformation and obstruction the law erects in such situations. Some have overcome these hurdles and been reimbursed small sums. After the Lords ruling the women could no longer be arrested for trespassing the base but only escorted off. However, when the authority of the state is thwarted its violence soon surfaces and the landowners' legal right to ask trespassers to leave by the most direct route has sometimes been interpreted by MOD police (on whose orders?) to mean let's use our superior strength to evict with violence.

The campaign against Greenham air base conjoined, although uneasily, local people, recreational walkers, lawyers and antinuclear peace campaigners, although with very different degrees of militancy, but agreed in their aim to see the common returned to the people. In June 1991 the 501st Tactical Missile Wing (Cruise missiles to you and me) left USAF Greenham and it became the property of the MOD again. The base is now virtually empty and unused and the longest runway in Britain is closed. Built on shifting gravel this runway was also the most expensive in Britain, so unstable it took millions just to keep it still. The commoners finally had their rights extinguished, although entitled to share in an £80,000 compensation fund, so the land is now freehold and there are strong suspicions the MOD plans to sell it to developers. But builders and buyers beware; shifting gravel and an unshifting determination by many to reclaim the common for everyone are still there.

17

The Lost Commons

The fight to reclaim Greenham Common from the military has rather overshadowed the continuing attempts to resist the loss of common land elsewhere to the industrial and agricultural developers. There was a time when much of the land was held in common, but kings and barons grabbed most of it and kept it for themselves or gave it to their followers as a reward for battles won. Most of the land became privately owned, so that now, if you want a piece to live on, you have to buy it back.

Today one and a half million acres of common land remain (4 per cent of the land of England and Wales), but it is all owned by someone. These commons are a relic of the manorial system, when crops were grown on the better soil and some of the people as 'commoners' had rights of access to the poor land unsuitable for cultivation, to graze their cattle. Sometimes they had other rights, such as pannage (the right to let their pigs eat beech mast or acorns), but God help the commoner who picked up the acorns himself or even shook the tree for his pigs; or turbary (the right to dig turf or peat for use as a fuel, but in his own house only). These rights were attached to the house or cottage and many survive today. Common land is normally unfenced, but on four fifths of it everyone except the commoner is technically a trespasser.

During the nineteenth century many owners of common land, especially if it was in or near a town, realised there were fortunes to be made from selling it for private development. All they had to do was get rid of the commoners, or at least buy them off. We are able to enjoy the landmarks and walk in the green open spaces today because there were activists who resisted such disposals, using a combination of local direct action and the law against such landowners and their lawyers. Courageous commoners, usually tenants of the local Lord of the Manor and often dependent on him for their livelihood, in alliance with middle class conservationists, who had in 1865 formed the Commons Preservation Society (CPS), now the Open Spaces Society, aimed to secure these open spaces for the use and enjoyment of everyone.

The battle for the commons was most intense in London because here the pressure on land was greatest. Earl Spencer, one of the new breed of developers, owned, as Lord of the Manor, Wimbledon Common and Putney Heath and planned in 1864 to sell off Putney Heath for residential building and use the proceeds to turn Wimbledon Common into a fine private park with a grand new house for himself. Unfortunately for him the commoners were themselves men of some wealth, power and influence, who quite liked living on the edge of the common and were able to spike his plans. Not every fight was so successful, the commoners of both Plumstead and Tooting Commons had little wealth or influence and the owners just fenced in the land and built on it. Octavia Hill's efforts to save Swiss Cottage Fields failed and it is now Fitzjohn's Avenue.

Berkhamstead Common was saved by an early example of non violent direct action, admittedly with the help of a heavy mob. It had been acquired by Lord Brownlow who bought out most of the commoners with small sums of money but failed to bribe the town with the offer of a 43 acre recreation ground. When the owner erected a five-foot high iron fence across two miles of the common, blocking numerous rights of way, the inhabitants of Berkhamstead

Faslane nuclear base

Photo Fay Godwin

Footpath across Lydd army training ground

Photo Fay Godwin

R.A. chair addressing rally at Milldale

Photo Fay Godwin

Duke of Westminster Estate, Forest of Bowland

Photo Fay Godwin

Faslane Peace Camp

Photo The author

Faslane Peace Camp

Photo The author

RAF Lakenheath – For access pick up phone

Photo The author

John Bugg (centre) at RAF Lakenheath

Photo *The author*

were furious. Advised that only a commoner could object, they found one with sufficient means and courage to take on the owner. A Mr. Augustus Smith, Lord of the Isles of Scilly, paid 120 navvies to go to the common one March night in 1866 and demolish the fence with minimal damage, laying the pieces on the ground in a heap, much to the astonishment of the owner's agent the next day.

Hampstead Heath, Hampton Court Park and Kew Gardens were all saved as open spaces and the rescue of Epping Forest was one of the great victories of the CPS. When the Rector of Loughton, as Lord of the Manor, fenced off some 1,300 acres he deprived the poor of the parish of their right to collect firewood. A man and his two sons broke through the fence and were sent to prison for criminal trespass. The full story of this and the other struggles can be found in an account of the early history of the CPS by G.J. Shaw-Lefevre. Here, it is sufficient to say that Epping Forest was finally fully restored to the public in 1882 in a ceremony carried out with ironic appropriateness by Queen Victoria, considering that the land had been originally stolen from the people to make a royal forest. The best known of present day actions is the attempt to regain free access to Stonehenge, but it remains surrounded by a high fence and barbed wire, with only very restricted entry to the site allowed.

Despite many successes, Britain's stock of unenclosed land has steadily diminished, with 40% disappearing between 1858 and 1958. In 1958 a Royal Commission proposed that all remaining common land be registered with guaranteed public right of access subject only to an effective scheme of management. Intended to save the commons, it was widely welcomed, but in many cases it achieved the opposite. Often, failure to penetrate the bureaucratic jungle to register a common left the land unprotected and vulnerable to enclosure by avaricious owners.

Another attempt to save the commons was made in 1986 when representatives of local authority associations, lanndowners, farmers, recreational and amenity bodies, set up the Common Land Forum. It was hardly a revolutionary body, but it did achieve a consensus that there should be a natural right to roam freely over all common land. Perhaps a little optimistically, they expected the government to legislate to this effect. The conservative election manifesto of 1987 did contain a promise to "legislate to safeguard common land on the basis of the Common Land Forum", but they didn't and it was not even mentioned in the

1992 manifesto. The government in the form of David Trippier, Environment Minister, having taken other advice, and in particular that of about 200 grouse moor owners called the Moorland Association, decided that in the interests of other existing users such access for walkers was not on. The excuse was the need to protect wild life, although no conservation body considers that it would be threatened. The reason really being the desire to protect the rights, reputations and especially the shooting profits of the grouse moor owners. Perhaps Trippier shoots? Having lost his seat he has the time.

18

The disappearance of Rhu Spit

If these jottings so often refer to the way the Ministry of Defence (MOD) interferes with simple recreational walking, it is not because I object to the existence of the armed forces, although I do, but because I object to the way the MOD takes more and more open land to play games with its tanks and guns. The result is high wire fences blocking footpaths and enclosing mysterious establishments, which according to Ordnance Survey maps do not exist. However this story is mainly about land used by picnickers rather than walkers and the MOD didn't want to put a fence round it, they wanted to abolish it. That's right, blow it up, blast it out of existence and not just for target practice either.

The land in question was Rhu Spit, a terminal glacial moraine shingle bank on the east shore of Gareloch in Dumbartonshire, which was a well known beauty spot, part of which had been designated a Site of Special Scientific Interest. The object of the exercise was to widen the Rhu Narrows near the entrance to the loch so that Trident submarines could pass through on their way to the Clyde submarine base at Faslane. The first of these was

THE DISAPPEARANCE OF RHU SPIT

launched in Barrow-in-Furness on 4 March 1992 and two or will it be three are to follow.

When, in July 1989, the MOD announced their intentions there was enormous local opposition with 1,000 people signing a petition against the proposal and Dumbarton Council rejecting the plan unanimously. Faslane peace camp near the entrance to the submarine base and the oldest in Britain maintained a permanent and continuous protest against the operation.

Although the MOD had stated that the spit would not be touched until the spring of 1990, they gave just two days notice that contractors would begin blasting and dredging at 8am on 22 January. The Peace Campers called a demonstration for this time but it was not until the following day that a barge arrived which the contractors planned to use to plant the explosives. It was guarded by MOD police in inflatables, but Faslane Peace Campers, Sea Action members and some local people, in four of their own inflatables, attempted to board the barge. The ensuing encounter was described in the March issues of *Sanity* and *Southern Resister*. According to *Sanity*:

> "A police inflatable rams a Sea Action inflatable against the Rhu Spit beacon breaking a demonstrator's nose. One person jumps into the police inflatable and arrests an MOD officer for breach of International Law. She is arrested and charged with breach of the peace. Another is handcuffed and charged with breach of the peace and common assault after he gets into the police inflatable and puts it into reverse."

During a subsequent sea action three people were arrested for breach of the peace and their inflatable was confiscated and towed away. It was returned the following day.

About the same time, at a meeting, MOD representatives were being reminded by a local district and regional councillor that two years earlier the Secretary of State for Scotland had given a promise that the Rhu Narrows would not be blasted. Whether the result of diplomacy, direct action, or both, the MOD cancelled plans to blast the Spit, deciding to do nothing until the Spring and then to use a dredger to widen the narrow entrance to the loch. They did however manage to destroy the beacon marking the end of the Spit. So please alter your O.S. maps, there is now only a little green buoy.

When Spring arrived, dredging started with the intention of widening the channel from 10.7 to 14 metres, by removing some

800,000 cubic metres of gravel and silt. They worked 12 hours or more a day using a large bucket dredger from Holland rather than a promised, and quieter, suction dredger, to the consternation of the inhabitants of the close-by and wealthy town of Helensburgh. The local council monitored the resulting noise and general disturbance to no avail. Don't ever underestimate those wily MOD civil servants, they knew what they were doing. The channel-dredging alternative to blowing up the Spit so undermined it, that it sank slowly into the loch and is now fenced off, for the protection of the public you understand.

This anti-Trident campaign has some local support but there are others who have tried to get rid of them by appealing to the Secretary of State for Scotland to revoke planning permission for the camp previously obtained from the local council, fortunately so far without success. The peace campers did not give up and have stepped up their campaign of resistance to Trident using Non Violent Direct Action techniques to great effect, despite being frequently arrested. Recent activities have included ambushing nuclear warhead convoys on their way to the Naval Armaments Depot at Coulport, blocking traffic entering Faslane submarine base and harassing the movement of naval ships in the loch using their small but fast inflatable boats, as they did HMS Vanguard, the first Trident submarine, on 25 October 1992 during its approach to Coulport.

Whether you are opposed to the Trident submarine base because you detest the military activities of nation states, fear the proliferation of nuclear weapons, or simply believe that the land belongs to the people and that even a small picnic site should not be destroyed nor suffer radioactive contamination, the Faslane Peace Campers in Shandon, Helensburgh, Dunbartonshire, Scotland, deserve your support.

19

About balls and pyramids

Remember the four-minute warning which in 1964 we were told would keep us safe, well, safer, and which was dependent on the missile early warning system at Fylingdales on the North Yorkshire moors? The three golf ball structures were visible for miles and did have an awesome beauty as well as providing a useful landmark in what is a popular area for walkers. The radiation produced there was probably not intense enough to be a danger to the health of ramblers.

Recently, however, these radar antennae were condemned as obsolete by the US military who are in control, to be replaced by a new phased array radar. This takes the form of a truncated pyramid 32 metres high, operational from the end of 1992. The more intense radiation generated from this device could be a health hazard, according to a British consultant on electromagnetic radiation, reported in the New Scientist (12 May 1990). Similar systems at Cape Cod in Massachusetts and Sacramento, California, have generated considerable concern over the health risks and scientific opinion is divided. But, of course, as the *New Scientist* headline stated "New system at Fylingdales is safe says the RAF". And how would they know when any ill effects might not be apparent for years?

Far bigger and getting still bigger, is the other US eavesdropping base at Menwith Hill where 18 golfball radomes and a small forest of scannners and antennae sprawl across part of Blubberhouses Moor near Harrogate, North Yorkshire. A recent £13 million expansion links it to several satellite systems and provides facilities to intercept international phone calls throughout the world – phone tapping without wires. But who still believes phone calls are private? Members of the Otley Peace Group, and others, visit the heavily guarded base regularly, eating in the canteen, enjoying the staff dance, even sitting inside the radomes. There were hundreds of these "peaceable incursions" in 1991 and one person was arrested 160 times. As with other bases, the anti-trespass military byelaws have been dubbed invalid by the courts and the footpath across Lakenheath US airforce base is not the only one the MOD have failed to extinguish.

The conflict between recreational and military needs for space in some of the most beautiful parts of this small island is continual and from North Yorkshire we turn to the Pembrokeshire Coast National Park in Wales where the MOD with the help and no doubt the insistence of the US Navy proposed to build an entirely new system of over-the-horizon radar on the disused St. David's airfield. This system, according to the same issue of the *New Scientist*, would bounce high frequency radio signals off the ionosphere (region of the atmosphere 60 to 300 kilometres above the earth's surface) down to an area 800 to 3,000 kilometres east and detect the signals reflected back from moving ships and aircraft inside this area. The proposed transmitting antennae would be spread over a kilometre or more and consist of 35 metal towers, 16 of which would be 40 metres high. They would emit sufficient power to expose people 200 metres away to an electromagnetic field strength which is on the borderline of the safety level set by the National Radiological Protection Board, a body not well known for setting really safe levels of exposure.

We are often told by government ministers that there is no evidence of danger (think of Sellafield) and this case is no exception. One way of making sure that there is no evidence is not to carry out any investigations. So you will not be surprised to hear that the MOD said that it had not conducted any research into the possible harmful effects of electromagnetic radiation and had no plans to carry out any such research. Others have, and some, although not all, studies found statistical evidence of suppression of immune function, cancer and eye problems associated with such radiation. Chinese studies of people living near radio antennae and radar installations have detected significant changes in immune function with exposure to much lower levels of radiation. A research worker at Surrey University studying the effects of this type of radiation on the brain was reported in *The Guardian* (5th April 1990) as saying that it is associated with an increased incidence of brain tumours and a possible association with leukaemia was being investigated.

Haverford West County Council responsible for approving planning applications in the National Park said it would consider the radar installation proposal on its merits, taking into account the anticipated environmental impact and the views of all interested local groups and individuals. Local residents started a 'Pembrokeshire Against Radar Campaign' (PARC). But as the proposed site was crown land the government had the power to impose the scheme if it considered it "in the interests of national security".

Now, the radar system may never be built. In April 1991 the plan was abandoned and we may never know why. Was it because of the anticipated scale of public protest and opposition, or had secret government research confirmed that such levels of radiation are dangerous, or, with an impending change of "enemy", would it have been just in the wrong place?

20

Menacing mountain hoppers

Few city dwellers still romanticise over the peace and quiet of the countryside, every living environment has its own aural template and tempo, and those who seek to escape the city, whether permanently or just from time to time, do so because they seek a healthier and more positive space to enjoy. But take care in your choice of countryside, citizen, or you may experience more than the sounds of industrial agriculture blending with those of the wild life, weather and livestock. Many rural communities are terrorised by the sudden ear-shattering screams of a Tornado, Phantom, Harrier or Jaguar passing overhead. Whether practising nuclear bombing runs (you may feel you are the target) or learning to fly under enemy radar, these terrible monsters may fly less than 100 feet above your head, would you believe, and emit up to 400 decibels of sound. They prefer pleasant valleys and flying between hillsides so what could be more suitable than the Lake District and Yorkshire

Dales national parks and, ironically, the Eden Valley. The north and west is littered with low-flying (down to 250 feet) zones and in much of north west Scotland, the Scottish borders and mid-Wales ultra-low-flying zones allow flying down to 100 feet. Pilots have been heard to boast that on the tops they go down to 25 feet, and who is going to stand up there with a tape measure, checking?

Farmers are concerned about the noise stress effects on their livestock, the ground can be polluted with toxic hydrazine vapour (lethal dose 1g), and the air with carbon monoxide, nitric oxides, hydrocarbons and sulphur dioxide, the products of kerosene combustion. Planes crash or collide from time to time and although the dozens of deaths in recent years have all been aircrew, eventually civilian involvement is inevitable and that means you the walker, agricultural worker or village resident. You may complain, and 5,600 a year have done so. Even some conservatives have complained, perhaps because it frightens the horses. In September 1989 the Ministry of Defence report on low-flying training by the Comptroller and Auditor General (£5 from HMSO but don't waste your money) stated that there was no alternative to the 151,000 flights a year, costing £304 million of your money, but suggested that the misery could be spread more evenly across Britain. Thank you very much but we would prefer it to be concentrated over the Houses of Parliament and Downing Street. As the complaints continued, a House of Commons Select Committee said in May 1990 that low altitude manoeuvres should be bannned, there should be tighter controls on the 55,000 hours of flying between 250 and 600 feet and flying under 250 feet should be phased out. Not a lot of notice was taken of that. Complaints have been ignored and demonstrations difficult to organise here. German demonstrators' success in the Autumn of 1989 resulted in a NATO exercise being transferred to the Highlands of Scotland using RAF Lossiemouth as a base. As the arrogant MOD pointed out, it didn't make all that much difference to the total annnual flying hours.

When an order for 33 Tornado combat aircraft was cancelled it did not mean fewer training flights, because they were only intended to be mothballed as reserves "to replace those lost in accidents or as a result of enemy action". CND campaigned in 1990 against all this, and designated July 1st to 8th in Scotland and July 8th to 15th in England as low-flying weeks. Bet you didn't even notice. But it was ironic to read in March 1991 of a ban on low-flying over Highgrove House in Gloucestershire.

Then came the Gulf war. Yorkshire residents near RAF Leeming were asked to put up with more low-flying (did they have a choice?) because, of course, the lads had got to practise a bit more now. Elsewhere, people were not even asked. Nevertheless, support for the campaign against low-flying evaporated; replaced by jingoistic acclaim, across most of the political spectrum, for "our boys" and their need to practise the techniques which proved so effective in killing Iraqi civilians and conscripts. After the Soviet Union, a new bogey is needed. In the short term Saddam Hussein has been useful, but who will be Oceania's new enemy?

21

Hooper's hedge hypothesis

Hooper's hedge hypothesis states that the number of species of tree or shrub in a randomly selected 30 yard length of hedge gives roughly its age in hundreds of years. Find three species and the hedge is about 300 years old. Try it out, but don't leave it too long, because England's hedges are fast disappearing. It is one way of identifying the transformation of the landscape that occurred during the 17th, 18th and 19th centuries. During this period the open field system with its vast fields of up to several hundred acres was being converted into small hedged fields of 5 to 50 acres. This process was until 1660 ineffectually opposed by the government of the day, but after the restoration of the monarchy and the institution of a government of landlords, the process was speeded up by the use of Parliamentary Acts of Enclosure, so that, especially between 1750 and 1850 and in the Midlands, the rural landscape and way of life suffered a drastic change.

The manorial landlords, wishing to make money out of large scale sheep and cattle farming which needed little labour, achieved economies of scale by enclosing much common land used by the peasants for grazing their cattle and dispossessing them of the strips of land they cultivated under the open field system. Many villages were left deserted and the evicted peasants and their families had little choice but to move to the towns. This is where capitalism began, in rural England. The peasants either found jobs in the factories of the early years of the industrial revolution or were reduced to street begging.

This process is described in enough detail in the history books but little space is given to the plight of the peasant families who lost the land they cultivated or used for grazing, in fact about as much as is given to the problems of the fox hunting gentry who were inconvenienced by the new solid obstacles blocking their path. Here English compromise triumphed as thorn hedges became the norm, easy to jump on horseback but effective in containing the landowner's livestock. In upland areas with poor soil drystone walls were an alternative.

This is a plea for the retention of the bocage or hedgerow landscape for the richness and variety it provides, valued for recreation by town and country. There is little pleasure in walking through the monotonous and desolate hedgeless landscape of intensive monoculture farming. But the countryside is not just for tourists and the large scale agricultural capitalists have turned against hedges, grubbing them out at an alarmingly increasing rate. Poor or non-existent management is now contributing to the loss.

A survey, carried out in 1991 by the Institute of Terrestrial Ecology for the Department of the Environment, found that 25,000 miles, over 10%, of the hedging existing in 1984 had been lost by 1990. Others have calculated that in the 1980s the annual rate of loss increased from 2,900 to 4,000 miles with 120,000 miles gone in the last twenty years, or over a mile per daylight hour. In March 1992 the environment minister David Trippier, just before he lost his job and his parliamentary seat, talked of the need for legislation requiring farmers to notify any intended removals of hedgerow (including cases of sorry but the chainsaw slipped?) and of help (money?) to the farmers to put back the hedges they had removed in the first place. A profitable sideline that could go on for ever.

Loss of hedgerow is most complete in East Anglia which had already lost half its hedges by 1980, to produce open prairies interrupted only by barbed wire or electric fencing, in which not just hedges but banks, trees, ditches and pools have disappeared with a corresponding massive destruction of wildlife habitats. The practice of maximising cereal yield to benefit from an artificially high subsidised price has resulted in the loss of all other forms of land use, as marsh, meadow, fen and woodland have been destroyed. For such a farmer a dense network of hedges is an obstacle impeding mechanisation; wasteful of arable land and of time in the upkeep of field boundaries. Subsidies, running at a yearly rate of five billion pounds, have encouraged overuse of fertilizers and the longer result of soil erosion leading to dustbowl conditions and nitrogen contamination of underground water resources.

It is not nostalgia for a romantic past nor automatic rejection of economic change that is behind a plea for the retention of the hedge. A walker is not equipped to specify good agricultural practice but can hope bad practice does not destroy the pleasurable downland landscape. There is support for the hedge however, and from an unlikely source. The bureaucrats of the Council of Europe have published a treatise on hedges by the French-Swiss Jean-Pierre Biber who argues that there are agronomic advantages in the well placed hedge because it helps to maintain the balance of the rural agricultural environment. The biological value of its contribution to the landscape is self-evident, but he also spells out the economic advantages. These include the windbreak effects which restrict damage to crops and reduce soil erosion. Hedges also retain water which reduces soil erosion, especially on slopes. He claims that overall crop yields are increased as the slight decrease near the hedge is more than compensated for by the increased yield over the main area of the field. He might also have mentioned that removing hedges destroys the breeding ground of the spiders and beetles that prey on many agricultural pests.

Until this century and in spite of the large population increase the land has been protected from erosion by good farming practice involving grazing, manuring and crop rotation. Now soil erosion is increasing due to bad practices such as the widespread sowing of the newer autumn cereals for the higher yields and bigger profits (Robert Evans, *New Scientist*, 7th July 1990) which leave the soil vulnerable in winter when the vegetation provides little cover. The soil of the land is one of our most important resources and with nearly 70% of the land in Britain owned by just over 1% of the adult population it is neither being conserved nor cared for.

22

Don't trust the National Trust

Disaster struck at the 1990 Annual General Meeting of the National Trust for places of Historic Interest or National Beauty (N.T.) when the members defied a recommendation of the Trust's ruling council for the first time since it was formed in 1895. The event was serious enough to warrant an editorial comment in the *Daily Telegraph* "...casts a poor light on a once highly respected organisation". The members had voted in a referendum, to ban deer hunting on National Trust properties from the following August, and this despite a call by the *Hare and Hounds* to their readers to join N.T. to prevent such treachery; and its call for the cancellation of the 194 fox hunts on the first day of the hunting season so that their supporters could go to to Llandudno to lobby the meeting. However, a separate resolution to ban fox, hare and mink hunting was defeated, but by a much smaller margin than in 1988.

So, did this mean that stag hunting would be banned and the 500 years of hunting by the Quantock Staghounds, for example, would end because they depend on the use of N.T. land in Somerset? Well no, because the council does not have to carry out the wishes of its members (just like parliamentary democracy) although the chairman (sic) Dame Jennifer Jenkins said that it would take "very serious account of the recommendations". The hunting community continues to press its arguments that hunting deer is good for the deer, that they clearly enjoy it and that the herds would not survive if hunting were to be banned. Apparently the farmers only tolerate the damage to crops caused by the herds because of the pleasure they obtain from hunting and would soon kill them all off if they could not be hunted.

Octavia Hill, the best known of the founder members of the N.T., wanted it to provide open spaces in the countryside for the enjoyment of town dwellers and the earlier work of the Trust was concentrated on buying land. It now owns over half a million acres, 1% of the country, much of it in National Parks and places of outstanding natural beauty, making it the second largest landowner.

However, in recent years it has become a safety net for preventing the decline and fall of the English stately house together with its contents, artefactual and human. Some 200 such houses are now in its possession and these have usually been donated by their owners, with or without a little money for their upkeep. A magnificent gesture you may think, visualising these gentry adapting to life in a high-rise council flat, but it isn't like that at all. They keep enough of the house for their own personal use, more than the rest of us ever need or enjoy, whilst the N.T. pays all the running expenses of the property and for the often extensive renovations needed. This is privatised social security, and at the top end of the market, financed by the two million members' subscriptions and donations which, in 1989 for instance, totalled forty three million pounds, placing it second in the top ten charities rating – just above Oxfam and below the Royal National Lifeboat Institution. Two years later, it came top, benefiting from over £55 millions in donations and pushing Oxfam into third place.

The uninhabited parts of the house are open to the general public, on certain days and at certain times, who pay to shuffle through these rooms, admiring the furniture and paintings, finally spending money on trinkets in the N.T. look-alike shops and refreshing themselves with N.T. taste-alike tea. You are asked to give money in the belief that you are making a positive contribution to conservation when it is more likely to be used to preserve properties from which the occupiers are the main beneficiaries.

Members have the right to elect fifty per cent of the ruling council (the other half is filled by nominations from other interested organisations) and those who wish to do more than use their membership to gain free access to N.T. properties are encouraged to devote time to voluntary work and fund raising, but certainly not to interfering with the ruling elite. The administration is filled with the less able but more snobbish sons and daughters of the establishment, who seem to think they can run a modern conservation body in a manner more characteristic of a feudal squirearchy. The fourteen regional committees who play a major role in running the Trust are dominated by large landowners and a proposal to have elected regional groups was condemned by the chairman as it could lead to a take-over by nutty factions with no interest in its true purpose!

An organisation, complacent in the face of criticism, which is secretive about the total number of its properties and the full extent of its estates, and even about some of its footpaths, which blocks public rights of way and fences off common land on its estates has no role to play in nature conservation and the recreational use of the countryside. It is a sacred cow whose time is right for slaughter.

23

An Obituary

The Nature Conservancy Council (NCC) was one of a miscellaneous group of organisations, sometimes called quangos, which are spawned from time to time by the government. Although given considerable independence they are expected to be dutifully obedient offspring and if they bite back they soon discover where power really lies.

The NCC was formed about 40 years ago, as a result of pressure from environmental groups, to provide the framework to protect the countryside and guide UK conservation policies. It was essentially a scientific body whose research into problems such as acid rain and industrial pollution has been well received, but it also advised the government and others on all matters which affected wild life and places and was responsible for designating, setting up and administering Sites of Special Scientific Interest, so keeping at bay some of the more mercenary development plans of industrial farmers, to the benefit of all who enjoy the countryside in their leisure time.

The NCC has now been dismembered as a result of a decision by Nicholas Ridley when Secretary of State for the Environment, who decided that it was becoming too "subversive". It has been broken up into separate organisations for England, Scotland and Wales with the Scottish and Welsh organisations (but not the English) being merged with their respective Countryside Commissions – agencies concerned with the recreational enjoyment of the countryside with particular responsibilities for "Areas of Outstanding Natural Beauty", long distance footpaths and National Parks. So since April 1991 we have the Scottish Natural Heritage and the Countryside Council for Wales, whilst the English rump is called English Nature.

Should this devolutionary step have received a cautious welcome for the measure of decentralisation involved, and if so why was it frantically opposed by over twenty leading independent environment organisations? Well, none of them was consulted before the changes were announced, but there was more to it than that. In its pursuit of conservation the NCC sometimes upset the development plans of large-scale farmers and those, regrettably including the Forestry Commission, who wanted to cloak the mountainsides of Scotland and Wales with conifer plantations, laid out with military precision. This is just what happened in 1987, probably sealing its own fate, when it opposed the afforestation of the Flow Country, a large flat area of peat bog in Caithness and Sutherland and an important breeding ground for some rare birds. This decision annoyed the powerful forestry lobby of big landowners who get large tax incentives to cover areas with conifers.

It was also true that the NCC in its Peterborough headquarters was seen by many Scots as a remote English bureaucracy that acted as though the whole countryside were just a scientific site and unable to appreciate rural reality and the local need to make a living from the land. The NCC had been particularly insensitive to the feelings of crofters and other small users of land of high conservation interest in Scotland. This produced just the opposition to the NCC as a whole which enabled the government, with the support of the anti-conservation lobby, to break it up and so please Scottish landowning, farming and forestry interests as well as the local political establishment and hopefully to win back some of the support lost to the Nationalists.

The myth that these changes were intended to improve conservation was dispelled when a leaked Treasury document confirmed that they were merely for administrative convenience. Certainly many more administrators have been appointed and the new Scottish and Welsh bodies are firmly under the control of the corresponding Secretaries of State, thus ensuring that the interests of large landowners, industrial farmers and blood sports enthusiasts are not interfered with. One NCC scientist was suspended in 1990 for pointing out in an article in *The Guardian* how well these interests were represented on the governing council of the NCC at the expense of conservationists. This had been achieved by packing it with pro-government appointees and not reappointing those opposed to NCC reorganisation, so ensuring that the ruling council supported these changes. Most of the staff were opposed but they were another group not involved in the decision making.

Observing such manipulations an anarchist can do little, other than at local level, but sit back and quietly wonder at it all. And, not least, wonder why the cost of advertising the new post of Chief Executive of the NCC for England cost £15,500 pounds, exclusive of VAT.

References

1 Common Roots: *Legg, Rodney* (1991) The Open Spaces Society
2 Forbidden Land: The Struggle for Access to Mountain and Moorland: *Stephenson, T.* (1989) Manchester University Press
3 On Common Ground: *Reed, Francis* (1991) Working Press
4 Our Forbidden Land: *Godwin, Fay* Jonathan Cape
5 This Land is Our Land: The Struggle for Britain's Countryside, *Shoard. Marion* (1987) Paladin Grafton Books